Geocaching: Basic Beginner's Guide

Vince Migliore

Blossom Hill Books

Title ID Number: 4465715

Title: **Geocaching: Basic Beginner's Guide**

Description: **Geocaching: Basic Beginner's Guide** is a step-by-step guide for getting starting in the hobby of geocaching.

ISBN-13:
978-1492873778

ISBN-10:
1492873772

Primary Category: Sports & Recreation / General
Country of Publication: United States
Language: English
Search Keywords: geocaching, guide, how-to, treasure hunting
Author: Vince Migliore

Blossom Hill Books
113 Sombrero Way
Folsom, California 95630 USA

Reorder: https://www.createspace.com/4465715

First Edition, October, 2013

Table of Contents

Acknowledgements

Several people helped with this book, including fellow geocachers Lynjer7 and Linda#1. Mary Pessaran provided editing support and Charlayne Mattingly offered enduring encouragement.

Cover photos

The front cover shows a cap with the Geocaching.com logo on the front and the GPS unit that helped me find this cache. This geocache type is known as a virtual cache, in this case a memorial plaque that has no log book. Virtual caches are being phased out. The rear cover shows a particularly devious hiding spot; a fence post where the top few inches swivel out to reveal a hole in the post which contains a film canister with the logbook inside. It's these kinds of puzzles and clever hiding spots that make the hobby so much fun.

1.   What is Geocaching?

Congratulations!

You're about to discover why geocaching is one of the fastest growing hobbies in America! Geocaching combines the fun of treasure hunting with the benefits of outdoor activity and the mental challenge of problem solving. Just where is that cache hidden? Follow the clues, navigate to the cache site, and match your wits against the clever person who hid the prize.

What is geocaching?

Geocaching.com, the most popular website supporting the hobby, defines geocaching as "a real-world outdoor treasure hunting game. Players try to locate hidden containers, called geocaches, using GPS-enabled devices and then share their experiences online."

The three key points are:

- It's a real-world outdoor game. You have to get out to a park or a bike path or some secret location to find the cache.
- You search for a treasure, or geocache (pronounced GEE-oh-cash). The cache itself is usually a small box or container that holds a log book and sometimes trade items, such as toys and trinkets.
- You find the prize by looking in the area referenced by latitude and longitude coordinates. Most people use hand-held geo-positioning satellite (GPS) devices but you might also use internet map sites or smart-phone apps to find the exact location

Technically, you don't *need* a GPS device because you can look up the coordinates on a mapping site, such as Google Earth, and get pretty close to the right location, where the container is hidden. Having a hand-held GPS device, however, makes the search much easier. You can also use smart-phone apps in place of a GPS device, but they are not as accurate.

Why is it so much fun?

There are as many reasons people get hooked on this sport. Some folks like the mental challenge of solving the puzzle of where the cache is hidden. Others like to combine the game with hiking, bicycling, or other outdoor or fitness activities. Youngsters and the young-at-heart love to open the box and see what's inside that they can trade.

Once you get started, however, the hobby becomes more enjoyable; it grows on you! You meet friends; you engage in friendly competition; you start hiding your own caches, and you get involved with the different aspects of geocaching. There are educational Earth Caches, rough terrain caches, difficult to solve puzzles, and a variety of challenges.

How is it played?

The basic procedure for playing is to look at a map of geocaches in your area. You find such maps on line. The prime hobby site is Geocaching.com, where you can enter an address and see all the caches in that neighborhood. The caches are rated by difficulty and terrain. You choose a few nearby caches, download the cache description and coordinates to your GPS device, then start driving or hiking to the cache site. The exact location where it is hidden is called **ground zero**. Once there, it takes some skill and detective work to find the cache.

For example, the coordinates might lead you to a pine tree. The tree has several pine cones hanging from it, but one of them looks like it's made out of plastic. This in fact is the man-made cache container disguised to fit in with its surroundings. The container is hollow and opens up to show the log book. It takes a sharp eye to locate it. The cache can be hidden inside a knothole of a tree, concealed within a fence post, or magnetically attached to the bottom of a metal object. This is where your detective skills come into play.

Sometimes you can get to within 100 feet or so of ground zero and then realize your path is blocked. You may have to back-track and approach it from another angle. Even at ground zero (GZ) you may have difficulty.

Once you find the cache, you open it up and sign the log book. If you find something inside to trade, you replace it with your own donation of equal or greater value. Some people leave a trademark or **signature item** to show others they've been there. You might also find a **travel bug** or **geocoin.** These you can take, but not permanently. They are designed to move from one cache to another. **Figure 1** shows a typical cache container.

Figure 1. This is a typical plastic cache container with a travel bug (left), a geocoin, and a small folded log book inside a plastic sleeve.

Finally, you close up the cache, replace it as you found it, and then head home to document your conquest. Go back on line to the cache website and record the caches you found, or didn't find. The geocaching websites keep a record of the caches you've completed, including their difficulty and terrain ratings.

2. Learn the Lingo

In order to play the game of geocaching you need to learn some of the language. These terms are fun and easy. You may have picked up a few already from **Chapter 1**. These words evolved from the long history of geocaching.

Most important terms

The most important words to learn are summarized here. A longer list follows.

It's best if you become familiar with these most common words and then look up the others later when you come across them.

A *geocache*, or *cache*, is the name used for the container or the exact location where it is hidden. A *geocacher* is a person who is looking for the hidden containers. Sometimes the geocacher is called a *cacher* for short. You might say "The geocacher hid his cache inside a hollow log."

Geocaching refers to the entire hobby of looking for caches. Geocaching can also mean you are going out to look for some caches. People who know nothing about geocaching are called *muggles*. The Harry Potter books refer to muggles as ordinary people or non-wizards. The terms have been adopted by the geocaching community. "I'm going out geocaching with two other cachers. We are taking along a muggle to show him how it works."

Sometimes people find a hidden cache by accident. Occasionally they will remove or empty out the container, not knowing that it's part of a game. This is what you call being *muggled*. "I hid a geochache but it got muggled."

Coordinates are the latitude and longitude that describe where the geocache is located. Latitude and longitude are used in mapping and navigating to pinpoint an exact spot on the earth. That spot is called *ground zero*, or *GZ*, in geocaching.

If a cache is hidden in a grassy field and several people have already found it, they may have trampled the grass so much that you can see exactly where they walked. This tell-tale marking on the ground is called a *geotrail*. "I found the cache easily. The geotrail led me right to ground zero!" See **Figure 2**.

Glossary

Archive: To discontinue a cache. It is removed from the Geocaching.com website.

Attribute: A pre-defined description of conditions surrounding a cache. Attributes use little pictures, or icons, on the cache web page to tell you what to expect. It includes such things as whether there is parking nearby, or if it is accessible by wheelchair. There are icons for hazards too, such as poison oak or ticks in the area. The Geocaching.com website has a complete description at: http://www.geocaching.com/about/glossary.aspx.

BYOP: Bring your own pen. Many caches are too small to hold a writing implement. If you want to sign the log you will have to bring your own pen.

Cache: This is the same as Geocache; a container holding a logbook and possibly other items.

Cacher: A person who engages in geocaching.

CITO: Cache In, Trash Out. This is an operating principle for all geocachers. If you find a cache that has trash around it, make a genuine attempt to clean it up. Some events have that clean-up process as the main focus of the cache, so that participants will bring trash bags for a major clean-up. A CITO is also a type of cache where participants include environmental clean-up as part of the cache adventure.

D/T: *Difficulty and Terrain*. Geocaching.com rates caches on the overall difficulty of finding the cache, on a 1 to 5 scale, and the terrain, from flat ground to mountain climbing, or special equipment needed. A cache that is in plain sight might be rated difficulty 1, while a hollowed out pine cone on a tree full of pine cones might rate a 4 in difficulty. A bike path, where you can walk right up to the cache might have a terrain rating of 1, but one where you need a canoe to reach an island would be rated 5 difficulty.

Difficulty: See D/T. This is the overall difficulty of finding the cache.

DNF: Short for Did Not Find. When you fail to find the cache you can log a DNF on the cache web page.

EarthCache: An EarthCache is one that has a geologic, scientific or environmentally significant story to tell you about the Earth. Generally there is no physical cache or log book to sign. Instead, you send answers for specific questions to the cache owner in order to qualify to log the cache. A meteor crater is a good example of an EarthCache. You might find a plaque or poster that describes the area. Questions for such a cache would be "When do scientist think this meteor struck the earth," or "How much did the meteor weigh?" You need to answer these questions correctly to qualify for logging the cache.

EventCache: A one-time meeting of geocachers. Cache events often have a theme, such as a holiday celebration or a costume party. The event sign-in sheet becomes the log and the cache is archived right after the meeting.

First-to-Find: This is a prize – the honor of saying you were the first one to find a cache when it was newly listed. If you are the first geocacher to locate the cache you will find a blank log and you will get the FTF "honors." Some geocachers are competitive and strive to be the first to find a cache. On occasion, the cache owner will leave a specific prize for the FTF person.

FTF: See First-to-Find.

GC code: Geocaching.com assigns a unique code number to each listed cache. The code number appears in the upper right corner of each cache web page. Geocaching.com codes begin with GC; example, GC4F81V is one of the author's cache code numbers.

Geocache: The geocache is a container that holds a log book which you sign when you find it. It may contain toys and trinkets (called SWAG), or trading items, such as travel bugs and signature items.

Geocacher: A person who is engaged in geocaching.

Figure 2. A typical "geotrail" where the grass is trampled leading up the hill to the cache site.

Geocoin: A coin or emblem that is traded by placing it in the geocache. The geocoin is numbered and tracked on geocaching sites. The owner of the geocoin can look up where it has traveled and who has moved it.

Geotrail: A marking on the grass or earth which shows that human traffic has passed by and may indicate the cache location. See **Figure 2**.

GPS: Global-Positioning Satellite. GPS is a hand-held or automobile based device that uses satellite signals to determine your current latitude and longitude.

GPX: A data file containing all or most of the information describing a geocache. It is downloaded from a web page and stored on your GPS device.

Ground Zero: The exact location, defined by latitude and longitude, where the cache can be found.

GZ: See Ground Zero.

Latitude, Longitude: Latitude and longitude are the imaginary lines that crisscross the globe and make it easier for people and ships to navigate to a specific location. There are different ways to write these numbers but for geocaching the most common form is to use degrees and minutes with three decimal places for the minutes, such as N 40° 46.152 W 073° 58.689. This is the standard format for geocachers. The same location can be written with degrees, minutes, and seconds, and it takes the form: N 40° 46' 09.120" W 73° 58' 41.340".

Letterbox. A Letterbox is a variation on the traditional geocache. It was a sport invented before the use of the GPS system and employs a description, a map, or a puzzle that has to be solved in order to find the treasure. It has now been incorporated into the broader-based geocaching hobby. The Letterbox contains a log book and a rubber stamp with a stamp pad. Letterbox players carry their own stamp and log book to the location. They use their own personal stamp to leave an impression on the cache logbook, as well as using the Letterbox stamp to mark their own personal log book. This way, both the Letterbox owner and the Letterbox players collect impressions of each other's stamps.

LPC: An abbreviation for the log: Lamp Post Cache. Most lamp posts have a metal skirt around the base to cover the retaining bolts. This cover can lift up and provides a common hiding place for a cache.

Multi-cache: A two-part or multi-stage geocache puzzle. You might use your GPS device to navigate to the first stage, where you will find further instructions or coordinates to direct you to another location.

Mystery cache: A mystery cache, or puzzle cache, is a form of geocaching where you have to solve a puzzle or riddle to find the final location. An example is to provide starting coordinates then ask the player to answer questions. Example: What year was President Obama born? Add the last two digit of that year to the North coordinates and subtract it from the West coordinates. The revised coordinates indicate the final Ground Zero. Puzzle caches can get quite difficult, but they provide a unique challenge.

Offset cache: See Multi-Cache

Puzzle cache: See Mystery cache.

Signature item: A signature item is something with your name, or more often your geocaching name, that you leave inside a cache to show you were there. People often make up their own signature items, such as a wooden nickel disk with their name stamped on it, or a hand-painted rock. Some people buy special-purpose signature items such as small metal coins, business cards, or personalized stickers that they leave in the cache.

SL: *Signed Log*: an abbreviation used when logging your visit on the cache web page log.

Spoiler: A photo or description that gives away the location of the cache. If a cache is hidden behind a loose brick in a wall, the spoiler might say "Third brick from the end, six rows up." A spoiler will destroy the challenge of finding the cache, but sometimes the searcher is in a hurry.

SWAG: Stuff We All Get. This is a term derived from the donations that celebrities get for attending public events. For geocaching it translates into the toys, trinkets and (well, let's be honest) "junk" that people leave for trade or give-away in the cache container.

Terrain: or Terrain Rating: This is the level of difficulty, 1 to 5, for the pathway or conditions for getting to the cache. A sidewalk on level ground would be a terrain rating of 1. If special equipment is required, such as a ladder or a rope, the Terrain Rating would be higher, such as 3.5. The most difficult caches, where you need mountain gear or a boat, will go as high as 5 on the difficulty scale.

TFTC: Abbreviation for the log: "Thanks for the cache."

TFTH: Abbreviation for the log: "Thanks for the hide."

TOTT: Abbreviation for the log: "Tricks of the trade," or "Tools of the trade." Example: Many metal fence posts have a rounded cap on top. Experienced cachers like to glue a box or film canister inside the removable cap. This is a trick of the trade. ***Tools of the trade*** are common items used to help you find or retrieve the cache. This includes sticks with a magnet or hook on the end, a mirror, a compass, a telescoping pole, or a set of tweezers to remove the log from a tight container.

Traditional Cache: This is the normal cache described by coordinates and it's the one and only location. There are no puzzles to solve or stages to go through.

Travel Bug: Travel bugs are toys, figurines, coins, or emblems that have a tag with a tracking number so the owner can follow where the bug has been. The travel bug is not kept by the geocacher, but is instead transported to another cache. It can travel all over the world.

UPR: An abbreviation for the log: "Unusual Pile of Rocks." This is given as a clue or spoiler for others to help find the cache.

Virtual Cache: A cache that does not have a log book to sign or a container to find. A statue of George Washington might serve as a virtual cache. In order to verify that you found it you would have to send information to the cache owner proving you were there. This is generally a set of questions that you can answer by visiting the virtual cache. Example: What year was the statue placed there? Who was the sculptor?

3. Before You Start

Make a plan

The old scout motto is "Be Prepared." Before you go for a hike you have to know where you're going, how far the hike is, and if you'll need any special equipment, like a compass or a map. The same kind of preparation is needed before you start geocaching.

The basic strategy to begin geocaching is:

1. Find the map which shows where the geocaches are hidden in your neighborhood. You find that map on line using a computer. You must pay $30 for a Premium Membership on Geocaching.com to see the maps.

2. From the map select two or three caches that fit your needs. As a beginner you may want to pick caches that are nearby, easy to get to, and easy to find once you get there.
3. At the cache site you will need to retrieve the container from its hiding place, sign the log, and if you so desire, exchange a trade item.
4. Replace the cache and make it back home safe and sound.

Let's take each of these steps in turn and fill in the details. This is a heads-up that will help prepare you for your first outing.

Find the map

Geocaching.com is the most prominent on line resource for geocaching. This website has everything you need to get started and keep you moving in the sport. Take a look at **Figure 3**, which shows the main page. You will eventually use this website to find and download caches to your GPS device. Other geocaching sites are listed in the Appendix.

Figure 3. This is the page heading you will see when signing up for a Geocaching.com account.

Step-by-Step:
Open an account

1. [ ] Sit down at a computer or tablet that has access to the internet.

2. [ ] Open your browser, such as Microsoft Explorer, or Firefox.

3. [ ] Navigate to www.geocaching.com.

4. [ ] You will see the opening page for Geocaching.com as illustrated in **Figure 3**.

5. [ ] Take your time to think of your geocaching nickname. This name will be with you for a long time, so choose something cute or memorable.

6. [ ] Click on the **CREATE A NEW ACCOUNT** box at the center right side of the page.

7. [ ] You'll see the Member Registration page, **Figure 4**.

8. [ ] First box: Enter you geocaching nick-name, your Username. Again, choose wisely.

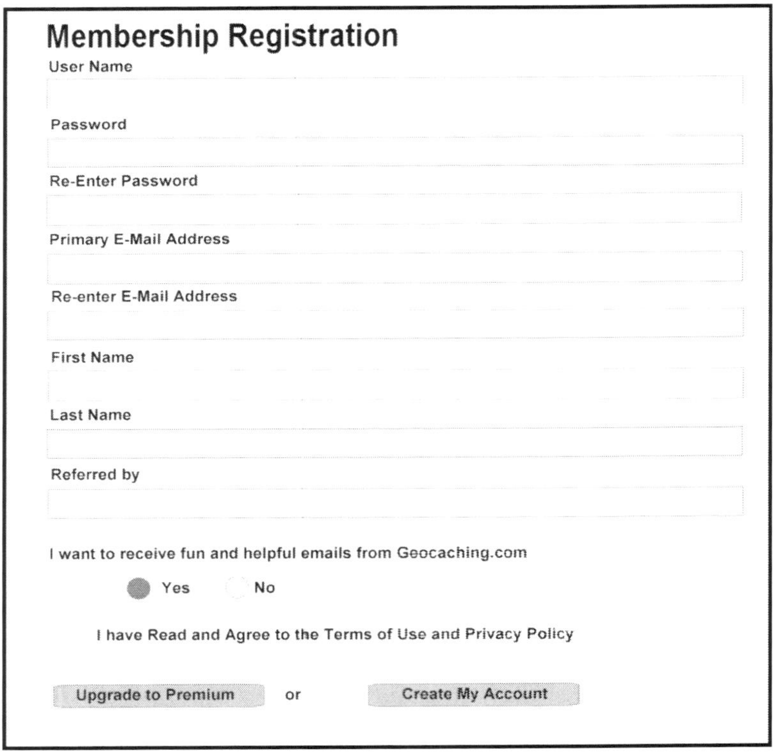

Figure 4. Fill in the Membership Registration page.

9. [ ] Second box: Enter an easy-to-remember password.

10. [ ] Save a written copy of your Username and Password.

11. [ ] Third box: Re-enter password.

12. [ ] Boxes four and five: Enter the email address where you will receive notices from Geocaching.com.

13. [ ] Boxes six and seven: Enter you name. It doesn't have to be your real name.

14. [ ] If a current member is helping you to register, you can add his or her geocaching name here, otherwise leave it blank.

15. [ ] Click on Yes or No for your choice of receiving email from Geocaching.com.

16. [ ] For the last box, click on the blue **TERMS OF USE** link and read the regulations.

17. [ ] Likewise, click on the blue **PRIVACY POLICY** link and read their policy statements.

18. [ ] Finally, click on the **I HAVE READ AND AGREE TO** . . . box, then click on the words **CREATE MY ACCOUNT**.

19. [ ] Sign up for a Premium account. It is only $30 for a year and it gives you all kinds of help and extras. Membership allows you to see the cache area maps needed for the steps that follow. Membership gives you more search options, statistical records, and more cache listings. Simply click on the **UPGRADE TO PREMIUM** link and fill out the form.

Select caches

After you've signed up with Geocaching.com you can see maps of caches in your area.

The plan here is to simply LOOK at the map, just to get an idea of how the game works. Once we find some geocaches nearby we can select a few for our first adventure. At this point we are assuming you do not have a GPS device and you do not have a premium membership to Geocaching.com.

Technically, you do not absolutely NEED a GPS device to find your first caches. What we want to do now is find a couple caches using a map service and then, if you are sure you like the hobby, you can buy a GPS later. This use of on line maps is a good tool to have even after you buy a GPS, because it makes finding the caches a lot easier.

Step-by-Step:
Selecting caches – home work

Selecting caches is a multi-step operation, but it is not at all difficult. With so many steps involved you might want to break it up into segments. Like learning to read a map, the process can be fun and educational.

1. [ ] Navigate to Geocaching.com.

2. [ ] This time you'll see the same image as in **Figure 1**, but now you can sign in by entering your Username and Password in the boxes at the top.

3. [ ] Click on the **KEEP ME SIGNED IN** box just below the Password box. Press Return.

   NOTE: If you do NOT click the **KEEP ME SIGNED IN** box then when you open the Geocaching.com page you will see the **SIGN-IN** box at the upper right of the page as shown in **Figure 1** .You will need to click on that link to sign in.

4. [ ] Once signed in, click on the down arrow just to the right of the **PLAY** tab across the top of the main page.

5. [ ] Select **HIDE AND SEEK A CACHE**. A new page will appear: See **Figure 5**.

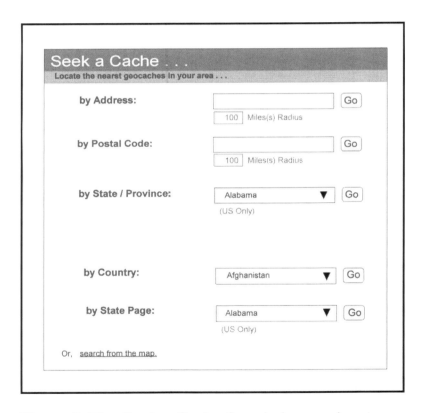

Figure 5. The Seek a Cache form helps you locate caches in your area.

6. [ ] Enter your street address in the first box and click the **GO** box. As an alternative you can enter your Zip Code in the second box.

7. [ ] A listing of all nearby caches will show up. Study **Figure 6** (Typical list). If this is your first time looking for caches you will see easy, beginner caches listed in bright green boxes.

8. [ ] Take a few minutes to study the list that appears for your neighborhood. Again, the bright green beginner listings are a good bet to look at first.

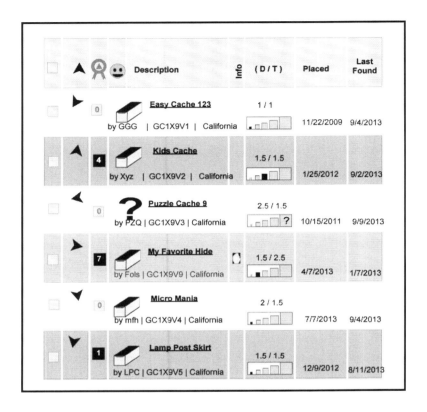

	▲	🏅	😊	Description	Info	(D / T)	Placed	Last Found
☐	►	0		Easy Cache 123		1 / 1		
				by GGG | GC1X9V1 | California			11/22/2009	9/4/2013
☐	▲	4		Kids Cache		1.5 / 1.5		
				by Xyz | GC1X9V2 | California			1/25/2012	9/2/2013
☐	◄	0	?	Puzzle Cache 9		2.5 / 1.5		
				by PZQ | GC1X9V3 | California	?		10/15/2011	9/9/2013
☐	►	7		My Favorite Hide	[]	1.5 / 2.5		
				by Fols | GC1X9V9 | California			4/7/2013	1/7/2013
☐	▼	0		Micro Mania		2 / 1.5		
				by mfh | GC1X9V4 | California			7/7/2013	9/4/2013
☐	▼	1		Lamp Post Skirt		1.5 / 1.5		
				by LPC | GC1X9V5 | California			12/9/2012	8/11/2013

Figure 6. This is a page of cache listings.

9. [ ] Examine each column:

a) Check-box column: Ignore this for now.

b) Distance column: This shows an arrow pointing to the direction of the cache from your home location and shows how far away it is.

c) Favorites column: This ribbon symbol shows

how many people voted for this cache as a
Favorite. This is a good indication of how
much enjoyment you will get out of finding it.
It is a little extra rewarding to find such caches.

d) Happy Face (Found) column. Once you've
found a cache and logged your find, a Happy
Face symbol will appear here. Since you are
just starting, these will all be blank so you can
ignore this column for now.

e) Description column: This column has several
different elements. The most important is the
Cache Type. For a beginner, you want to look
only at the **Traditional Cache** types
symbolized by a box with a green lid. The cache
name is listed as well as the GC code number.
Different types of caches are described later in
Chapter 9.

f) Difficulty and Terrain: The overall Difficulty
of finding the cache is rated on a scale from 1 to
5, with 5 being the hardest. To start, we want
choose easy-to-find caches, 2.0 or lower. The
same applies to the Terrain rating – keep it at
2.0 or lower. Caches higher than that may
require a tough hike, climbing rocks, or special
equipment. Again, as a newcomer, the website
will highlight in bright green the caches that
are good for a beginner. This column also
shows the cache size. The larger the size the

easier it may be to find, so look for the bigger ones.

g) Date placed: This is the date the cache was placed in the field.

h) Last found: The date showing the last time the cache was found is important. If the cache has not been discovered in over 6 months it may be missing or very hard to find. Stick with caches that have been found in the last six weeks or so.

10. [ ] Next, choose 3 or 4 caches that are near your house. Be sure to study all the factors listed in step 9 above. In summary, select ones that are easy to find (bright green listings). Select caches that are larger than micro if you can do so, and those that have favorite points, column 3. You may have to page down to see more listings. This is an important process, so take your time. You want to select caches that are relatively close to your home, easy to find and that have been found recently. Sometimes a bike trail or large park will have several good selections all near each other.

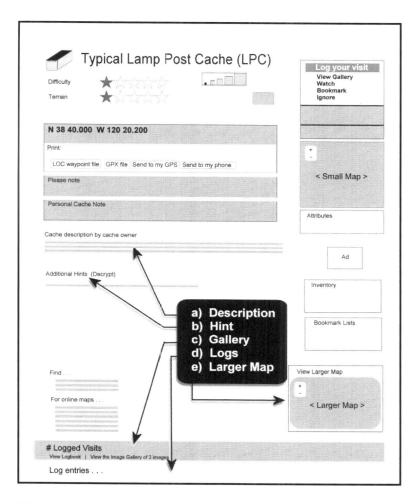

Figure 7. The cache description page is loaded with helpful information.

11. [ ] For each of your tentative cache selections click on the blue cache link. This will open a new page, the cache information page which includes a full description of the hide. As you read these instructions, track steps a) through e) on **Figure 7**. Get a note pad and start writing down anything that will help you once you're actually out in the field.

a) Read the description.

b) At the bottom of the description there may appear the words **ADDITION HINTS**. If there is a hint, click on **DECRYPT** to see the clue.

c) Below the description look for the **VIEW GALLERY** link. This too is in blue and underlined. The images (if any) often show the cache area and what the container looks like.

d) Below that, read the log entries of those people who have found the cache. These descriptions often include further hints to make finding the cache easier.

e) On the right side of the cache page you will see two maps. The top one is small, but if you scroll down you will see a larger map, with the words **VIEW LARGER MAP** at the top.

f) Click on the **VIEW LARGER MAP** link. A new page appears, **Figure 8** (typical).

g) On the new larger map page, use the slide control on the right to zoom closer into the cache. Above that slider, click on the **SATELLITE** box.

h) Now you will see a close up bird's eye view of the cache. If it's in your neighborhood you may already be familiar with the location. Zoom in closer using the slide control. You may see that the cache symbol is in a tree or near a lamppost. These are important clues for you. This is where your notes are crucial.

i) Zoom out again a little bit so you can get your bearings and see how to get to the cache site. It may require walking down a bike trail or walking through a park. This can be tricky because there may be a fence or a creek that you have to get around.

j) Take notes: write out the name of the cache and how to get there so that when you go into the field it will be familiar to you. You may want to print out some pages to help you. For example, you may want to print the map page. If you do print the map, click back to **MAP** view, as opposed to **SATELLITE** view before you print. It is easier to see on the printed version.

k) Make note also of landmarks near the cache site. Ground Zero might be just south of a telephone pole, or just north of a fire hydrant. You will need these clues once you are in the field.

12. If you've done everything right you should have 3 or 4 good opportunities to find your first cache(s). You should have notes or printouts for each one. By going through this process you will also have a good picture in your mind of where to go, what to look for, and how to get there.

Now you are just about ready for your first adventure.

Congratulations! If you got though all those steps you are about 95% up to speed for geocaching. Before you go out into the field, however, there are a few practical matters to consider.

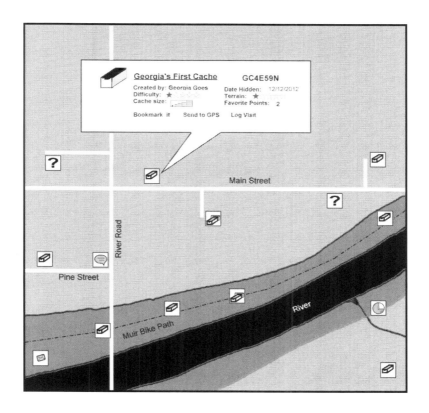

Figure 8. When you select the larger map you will see surrounding caches.

Are you old enough to go alone? Going with a friend is MUCH, MUCH better in many ways. Do you know what to bring with you? These questions will be addressed in the next chapter.

4. Go With a Friend

You are just about ready for your field trip. There are just two more matters to consider.

First, do you want to go alone or with a friend?

Going with a friend is generally much better. The hobby of geocaching is more enjoyable when you can share experiences with a friend. There are also some practical benefits. Two sets of eyes can find the cache much faster. Moreover, two people together are safer than one person alone.

Going with another newbie

A Newbie, or newcomer to the sport, is someone not yet familiar with the game. The advantage of taking a current friend or family member is that you know each other already, and you might both be interested in learning the game together. When two or more people work together, things just seem to go more smoothly. One person might be better at the computer work described in the previous chapters while another might be better at outdoor activities.

Going with an experienced geocacher

It's surprisingly easy to find another geocacher to go out with for your first run. It's important to set aside any shyness you might have because 99% or geocachers are thrilled and honored to be asked by someone to help with their first adventure.

CAUTION: Use common sense and good judgment if you decide to go geocaching with someone you don't know very well. While problems are extremely rare, it's best if you have all their contact information and let others know when you expect to go and return.

Step-by-Step:
Linking up with another geocacher

1. [ ] Go back to **Step-by-Step: Selecting caches – home work** (page 25) and repeat steps 1 through 8 to see a list of caches in your area.

2. [ ] For each listing, look at the names of the people who have made log entries.

3. [ ] As you go through the cache logs for the different listings you'll see many of the same names popping up for each cache. These are your neighbor cachers.

4. [ ] Look for names that indicate a family or team, such as "TeamWilson" or "The KatzFamily."

5. [ ] Click on the name in blue letters on the left side of their log entry. This brings you to their Profile Page

6. [ ] Look at their gallery – you may find pictures of people you can feel comfortable with. The **GALLERY** can be found on the 5th tab across the top of their profile page.

7. [ ] If you find someone who might be a good instructor, click on their email address on the left side of the page.

8. [ ] In the email message tell them what you're interested in; a little guidance in finding your first cache. The message might go something like this. "Hello neighbor. I am new to geocaching and I'm about to go out for my first cache. I see that you have experience in finding caches in this neighborhood. I wonder if I could tag along the next time you go? Better yet, I am looking to find cache XYZ. Maybe you could help me, or know someone who can help. Thank you in advance."

9. [ ] Then wait for the reply. It might take a day or two. If they cannot help they will often suggest someone who is more attuned to your needs.

10. [ ] Of course the experienced geocacher might suggest some changes to your plan. This is a matter for you to negotiate before your outing.

Important: Linking up with other, more experienced, geocachers may alter your plans considerably. The other geocachers may well want to engage in more advanced or rigorous activities, such as more difficult geocache challenges. Going with more advanced players will certainly speed up your learning process, but you have to weigh that against your own level of comfort. Do not be afraid to decline an offer. For example, if they are going on an all-day hike while you are looking for an easy one-hour adventure, then the goals of that group and your needs might not be a good match when you're first starting out.

What you need to bring

You should now have your papers for each cache. You should have a mental image of where they are located. Now you need to prepare physically for the first cache adventure. See **Figure 9**.

Things you will definitely need:

- Pen, pencil or other writing implement – so you can fill out the log.
- Good walking shoes and leg protection. You may have to squeeze behind a scratchy bush or walk through weeds, so don't wear sandals. Long pants will prevent scratches.
- A pair of tweezers. Some cache logs are tiny and may be hard to extract from the cache.

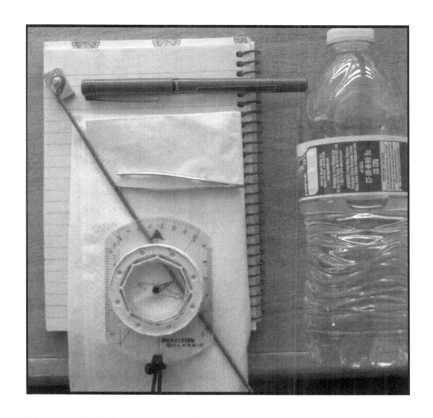

Figure 9. Bring support items with you. A few good things to bring are a pen and notebook, paper towels, tweezers, a compass, a probe with a magnet on the end, and water.

Things you might need:

- Small gifts or toys. This is necessary only if you intend to trade swag items if there are any inside the cache. See **Figure 10**.
- A local map.
- A compass.
- A cell phone.
- Water, both for drinking and cleaning your hands. Paper towels.
- Bug spray.

OK! If you've done everything in sequence up to this point you are ready for your first field trip. Nice job!

Figure 10. If you like the treasure hunting part of geocaching, bring items to trade or donate.

5. Your First Field Trip

Are you ready for you first field trip? It's a good idea to read through this entire chapter before you go out.

At this point you should have:

- The notes taken for each cache you plan to visit. This includes a map, the hints for finding the cache, and your mental images gained from studying the map aerial views
- Someone to go with, or a plan to go by yourself
- Sturdy outdoor clothing with good leg and foot protection
- The necessary supplies for logging the cache and trading swag items.

Remember to let someone know where you are going and when you expect to be back. Again, for this first venture you will not need a GPS device. We are planning on using the information gathered by looking at the Geocaching.com web page and the aerial view maps.

At the cache site

Once you're at the cache site look around for good hiding places. If you were going to hide a little box around here somewhere, where would you put it? Refer now to your notes and the landmarks you saw in the map aerial view. Was there a pole nearby? Did the hint indicate the cache was in a tree? If the description is for a Lamppost Cache, see if there is a pole around. The base cover of the pole, the skirt, may lift up to reveal the cache. If the cache is a *hanger* then look for a little box or cartridge hanging from the branches of the tree. If the description indicates "magnetic" then look for any metal objects it may be attached to. **Figure 11** shows what some of the typical cache containers look like.

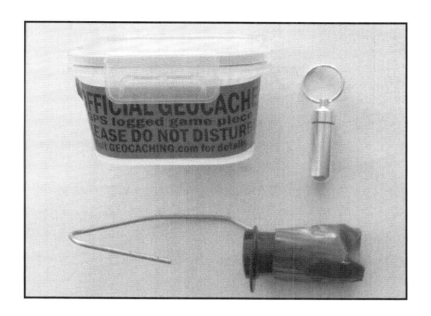

Figure 11. Typical cache containers include a sealed plastic food container, a bison tube, and film canister "hanger."

This is the fun part. You have to use your brain, your detective skills, and logic to discover the hiding spot.

The GPS satellite locating technology is only accurate to about 10 feet, so expand your search area. Put a rock or a mark on the ground where you think Ground Zero is, then walk around in a circle about 10 feet wide to find other possible hiding spots. Remember to look high and low. Geocaching rules require that you cannot bury a cache, so no digging should be involved, but the cache may be hidden by a rock, a log, or a camouflaged cover.

Still can't find it? Here are some ***Tricks of the Trade***:

- Look at the caps on any fence posts. These might lift up to reveal a cache site.
- Look at unusual rocks. Sometime the Cache Owner will drill a hole in a rock and hide things inside.
- Look for any metal objects; the cache might be stuck magnetically to the metal.
- Look inside tree branches. Many times the cache will have green tape on it.
- Look in knotholes in the tree or cracks in the wood of a telephone pole. Some caches are made of tape and slotted into the crack like a tiny envelope.
- Look for unusual signs or switchplates. Sometimes a sign is not real and pulls off just like a magnet, and the cache is on the back of the phony sign.
- Look for loose wire hooks or strings. Very often the cache is hidden inside a pole or down a pipe and you have to pull on the string to retrieve it.
- If the cache is in a field, look for trampled grass or a well-worn path. The previous geocachers may have left a trail.

If you and your partners still cannot find it, then stop and take a breath. Give it just one more quick mini-search. This happens only rarely, but it's usually just a matter of experience.

Do not spend so much time that you get frustrated. If two people cannot find the cache in about 20 minutes then do not be afraid to give it up for the time being. Remember, the object is to have fun, and you are just beginning, so let's try another one.

You should have a few other cache sites on your list that you can search. Go to the next one and start over. If you go through all your cache listings and cannot find one, then you always have the opportunity go back onto the computer, look up the cache description again, and write to the Cache Owner, or other geocachers, to give you a hint. They will generally provide some clues that will help you.

You FOUND it!

Yes! You found your first one! Congratulations!

OK, follow these steps:

- Before you open it up, stop for a second and memorize where it was hidden. You want to be able to put it back in exactly the same place when you are done. If there was a rock covering it, for example, make sure you don't throw the rock away.
- Look around. Make sure that no muggles are watching you.
- Examine the container. Does it have a screw cap? How do you open it?

- Open the container carefully. Sometimes it could have water or bugs inside if it was not sealed well.
- See what's inside. This is the fun part.
- Find the log book. This will be a folded or rolled up sheet of paper with the signatures of previous geocachers. Sometimes, for smaller caches, you may need a tweezers to extract the logbook from a tiny tube.
- See if there are any travel bugs, swag, trade items, toys or notes inside. If you have brought along your own trade items you can exchange one of yours, of about equal value, for one in the cache.
- If you see a travel bug and you want to help move it along, then you can take that too. Write down the travel bug tracking code.
- Sign the log. Use your geocaching name. You will see that most people write the date and their geocaching name. If the log book has plenty of space some people will write a quick Thank You or a smiley face just for the fun of it.
- Make a note to yourself describing what you found. If the log book is wet or there is dirt inside, you may want to enter that into your comments when you log the cache on the computer. If the cache is in an area with a nice view or if you find a well designed cache container, these are things you will want to write about when you make your report on the computer.

- If you have any of your own travel bugs, gifts, or swag that you want to leave then drop it in now. Do not put in anything so bulky that it will prevent you from closing up the cache again.
- Be sure the cache is sealed and return it to its original hiding spot.
- Be a good citizen and take out any trash that might be in the area.
- Review your notes one more time.
- Check your hands and clothing to remove any leaves, debris, or creepy-crawlies that may have landed on you.
- Head back home or to the next cache.

Nice job! Now you will head back home and record your finds, or Did-Not-Finds, on the cache web pages.

Make sure you get back home safe and sound.

6. Report Your Finds

Logging your finds

Logging your geocaching adventures creates a permanent record of your finds, and your attempts. Even caches that you were not able to find should be logged. Geocaching.com stores your statistics and keeps track of how many caches you have found. The website also tracks what kinds of caches they are, such as traditional caches or events you've attended.

On your first outing, you probably have a list of the caches you attempted to find. Now it's time to go back and record the results of your search. By logging all your finds and DNFs you can track your progress as you grow into the sport. You will find that you have more success at finding caches as you gain experience. You may also find that going with a group increases your success rate.

Step-by-Step:
Logging your finds and did-not-finds

1. [ ] Navigate to Geocaching.com.

2. [ ] If you're not automatically logged in, then click on the **SIGN IN** box at the upper right side of the screen.

3. [ ] Click on the **KEEP ME SIGNED IN** box just below the Password box if you want to stay logged in.

4. [ ] There a several ways to view the caches that you were looking for. The simplest way may be to select the second tab at the top which reads **YOUR PROFILE**.

5. [ ] Move your cursor over the **YOUR PROFILE** tab and click on **QUICK VIEW**.

6. [ ] You should see a list of the caches that you were considering, so you can click on the ones you want to make entries for.

7. [ ] If you don't see the cache name that you want to log, then go back to Geocaching.com, the main page and hover over the **PLAY** tab and select **HIDE AND SEEK A CACHE**. You

will see **Figure 5**. Then click on SEARCH FROM THE MAP on the right side of the screen.

8. [ ] Click on the name of the cache if you are using step 6, or click on the cache icon if you are using step 7.

9. [ ] The cache page shows up; **Figure 7** is typical.

10. [ ] Look at the upper right side of the cache page for the words LOG YOUR VISIT. Click on that.

11. [ ] A new page appears, **Figure 12**.

12. [ ] Move your cursor over the SELECT TYPE OF LOG pull down menu and select FOUND IT, DIDN'T FIND IT, or WRITE NOTE.

    a) If you found the cache, select FOUND IT.

    b) If you didn't find it but looked for a long time without success, then select DIDN'T FIND IT.

    c) If you didn't find it but you didn't really try too hard either, or if you think the failure was due simply to lack of experience, you might want to consider simply writing a note. You might say something like: "Didn't find it, but I'm new to this. I will try again soon."

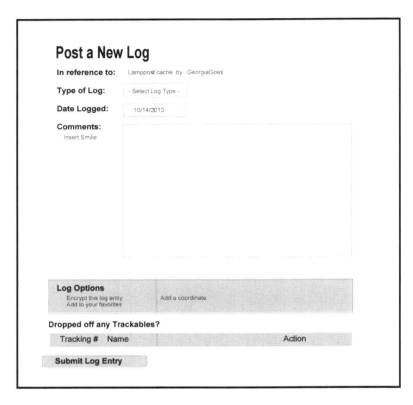

Figure 12. Fill out the Log Your Visit form.

13. [ ] In either case, write a little something about what happened when you were looking for the cache. Cache owners love to see notes about what people think of their caches. If the container was entertaining or decorative then say so. If the hide location offered a beautiful view then write that too.

14. [ ] There are no set rules on what you have to say in a log entry, but you should at least make note that you signed the log and you replaced the cache as you found it.

15. [ ] You should report if you left anything or took anything out of the cache.

16. [ ] If the log book or the container is damaged then say so in your comments.

17. [ ] Consider the etiquette and sportsmanship aspects of the log entry when you make comments. A brief entry might be simply "SL, TFTC" which means I signed the log. Thanks for the cache. How much more fun is it, however, if you give the log some pizzazz?!

Consider writing something like this: "Wow! Had a great time hiking on the bike path and viewing all the great scenery around. Found the well-crafted cache after about 2 minutes and opened it up to see lots of goodies inside. I took a wooden nickel signature item and left a small figurine of a cat. The log book is clean and dry. Replaced as found. Very enjoyable adventure; Thank you!"

That kind of log gives a shot in the arm to the cache owner and encourages other cachers to take the same hike along that bike path.

18. [ ] Check that the date on the log page is the actual date you made the find, or DNF.

19. [ ] If you found the cache and you picked up a trackable item, then you will have to log that; (see Circulating your own Travel Bugs, **Chapter 9**).

20. [ ] If you have your own trackable item and you dropped it off at the cache, there are boxes below the comments window where you can record dropping off your travel bug.

21. [ ] Click on **SUBMIT LOG ENTRY**.

22. [ ] Repeat the same steps for each cache that you found or did not find.

23. [ ] Congratulations; you are now an official geocacher!

Woo-Hoo! Give yourself a pat on the back!

If you enjoyed the adventure and you think you will get more involved with the geocaching, then it may be time to buy your GPS unit. That subject is covered in the next chapter.

7. Buying a GPS Device

Test run

The strategy we have been following is to find your first few caches using on line maps and paper records. Hopefully, this helped you get a feel for the activity. If you've found your first few caches and you think you are ready for a greater investment in the geocaching hobby, then it's time to think about buying a GPS unit to help with your searches.

GPS device options

There are several different GPS devices that you can use to find caches. Each of them has their advantages and disadvantages. You also have the option of not buying a GPS device and continue searching using the on line maps and paper notes that we've covered in previous chapters. If you do decide you want to buy a device there are many routes and techniques. These are:

1. GPS app on a smart phone or tablet.
2. Automobile GPS in a car.
3. Low-end hand-held devices
4. High-end (paperless) hand-held devices

Let's look at each of these options.

GPS app on a smart phone or tablet

Smart phones, tablets, and an increasing number of hand-held devices allow you to download programs, called applications or apps, which enable you to mimic the workings of a hand-held GPS device. These are available for iPhone and Android devices. Enter "geocaching GPS apps" on any search engine on line and you will see a long list of such programs. An app called "Geocaching" by Geocaching.com is available, for example, from iTunes for $9.99 (as of August, 2013). Likewise, Google Play offers a program called "C:Geo." The names, capabilities and costs of these programs change all the time, so it requires a web search to stay current.

The advantages of using a smart phone or portable device is that it's a quick and relatively simple way to get into the geocaching game – that is IF you already have a smart phone.

The disadvantages: The costs of using phone data programs where you are in effect surfing the internet as you search, can be pretty expensive. Another problem is that phone applications are not as accurate as a device that is made specifically for geocaching.

Dedicated GPS devices can link to several satellites at once so that the technology is much more accurate at pin-pointing your location. They have a very sensitive antenna built in, so they are far superior to the phone applications.

If you decide to use a smart phone, then you would start by looking at which programs are available for your phone or tablet. Use a search engine to find "Android geocaching apps" for example if you have an Android device, or iTunes if you have an iPhone.

Automobile GPS devices

Only SOME of the GPS units that are made for cars and trucks will work with the files you get from Geocaching.com. Some of the more expensive and advanced models allow you to download geocache locations to the car device. These are very handy if you are driving to most of your caches, but you would need the kind of unit that detaches from the car so you can carry it along a path or bike trail. For this reason it may be better to consider a hand-held GPS device that is made specifically for geocaching.

Low-cost hand-held devices

There are two broad categories of GPS devices that are made for geocaching, the low cost kind, and the *paperless* kind.

The low-cost units give you much of what you need for a fun adventure. As you may have noticed if you've already competed a geocache hunt, there is a lot of preparation necessary. You have to write things down, such as where the cache is located and its difficulty and terrain ratings. When you have a GPS unit, this information is loaded into the memory of the GPS and you can see the basic description and notes.

Even with this data, there are oftentimes things you still have to write down, such as the hints in logs written by previous visitors. The low-cost units provide you with all the basic information, such as the coordinates, the difficulty, and when it was last found. The more expensive paperless devices cost a lot more, but they hold a larger volume of the information that you see on the cache page. The file downloaded to this type of unit includes all the logs of previous visitors, which can help in finding the cache.

The Big Four manufactures for hand-held GPS units are Delorme, Garmin, Lowrance, and Magellan, in alphabetical order. These are the most popular manufacturers and reviews of their products can be found on the Geocaching.com website. You can also find reviews on shopping and auction sites, such as Amazon.com.

Some examples of entry-level geocaching units:

- Garmin eTrex 10: This costs about $100.
- Magellan eXplorist 110: About $120.
- Magellan eXplorist GC: About $130.

Examples of hand-held GPS devices are shown in **Figure 13**. There is also a low-cost device called the Geomate Jr., made for youngsters. It sells for about $60 and comes with geocaches pre-loaded on the device. There is some question about whether or not this unit will remain in production.

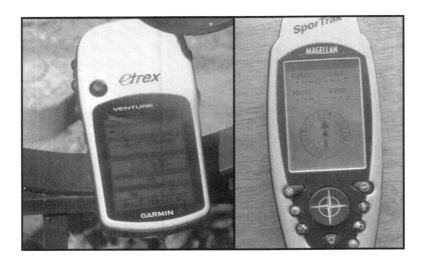

Figure 13. GPS devices for geocaching will generally fit in the palm of your hand

High-end (paperless) hand-held devices

The more expensive GPS units generally cost over $200, so buying one is a big decision. If you're a beginner, it's probably best to wait until you know a lot more about what features are important before you make such an investment.

The big advantage of the more expensive models is that they can hold just about all the information on a cache that you can see on the cache's web page. This includes its location, the full description, previous log entries, and the hint, if there is one. Photographs are usually NOT included in the file that is transferred to the GPS unit. A large memory allows you to download hundreds of caches in your area all at once.

The features to consider are:

- The map that comes with the GPS unit.
- The amount of memory it has.
- Pocket Queries – the ability to download many cache files at once.
- A USB connection to your computer.
- Screen size.
- Ruggedness, including waterproofing.

A thorough discuss of these are other points can be found at:
http://www.geocaching.com/about/buying.aspx.

8. After You Buy a GPS

Inspection

Congratulations on getting your GPS unit! Most units will need a battery and a memory card which are not always included. There are three things you have to do:

- Read the Instruction Manual.
- Read the Instruction Manual.
- Read the Instruction Manual.

No, that's not a typo, though it may be a bit of tongue-in-cheek teasing. Read the manual once through quickly to see the important areas of information. Read it again more thoroughly to be sure you understand everything. Finally, read it again focusing on areas of difficulty.

If you are going geocaching with friends, many of them may be able to guide you on how and when to use your GPS features.

Transfer software

No one tells you this, but the GPS is like a little mini-computer. You have to use specific software in order to use it. The software allows your computer to talk with the GPS unit. The software transfers the geocache files to your GPS device. Each manufacturer has its own dedicated program.

For example, the Garmin software download is at: http://software.garmin.com/en-US/gcp.html.

For Magellan:
http://www.magellangps.com/Magellan-Communicator-for-PC.

There are also third-party programs that work with multiple manufacturers.
See: http://www.easygps.com/, for Garmin, Magellan, and Lowrance.

The Geocaching website has a page which discusses different types of GPS software.
See: http://www.geocaching.com/software/.

These programs work automatically when you plug your GPS into the computer. You are now ready to download geocaching information, called GPX files, to your GPS.

- Most such programs will open up a window on your computer automatically once you plug the GPS cable in to the USB port. If that doesn't work with yours, then navigate to the program location and double click on it.
- Next, open a web browser to the Geocaching.com web page.
- Log in to Geocaching.com
- Click on the third tab **PLAY** menu and select **HIDE AND SEEK A CACHE**.
- On the middle right side of the page click on **OR, SEARCH FROM THE MAP**.

Loading caches

Once you've clicked on the **SEARCH FROM THE MAP** link, a diagram appears on your computer showing the many caches in your area. **Figure 7** is a typical example.

The idea today is to select 4 or 5 caches that are relatively near each other, and near your house, so you can make an afternoon adventure of geocaching.

Step-by-Step:
Loading GPS files

1. [ ] Connect your GPS to your computer using the USB cable. The computer should recognize your GPS device as described above.

2. [ ] Look around the map of your area. See if there is a park, a school yard, or a bike path that has several caches near each other. You may have to move the map around by clicking and dragging the mouse pointer.

3. [ ] As an example, let's say there are four caches along a trail in a nearby park. For each of the four caches . . .

   a) Click on the cache and look at the last date it was found. If it hasn't been found recently this is a sign of trouble. You may have to ignore it. The date of the last find is in the upper right corner of the most recent log entry.

   b) Likewise, if the last few logs show DNF (Did Not Find) that is a sure sign that you will not have success with this cache. Avoid caches that show **NEEDS MAINTENANCE**. These will have a little red wrench icon showing in the cache description.

c) Look at the difficulty and terrain ratings. Select this cache for your adventure only if you feel reasonably comfortable with the difficulty ratings.

d) Look at the size of the cache. Larger caches are generally easier to find.

e) Look at the number of favorite points the cache has. This is a good sign of an enjoyable adventure.

f) Click on the **VIEW LARGER MAP** link at the lower right map. Zoom in closer to view the cache and select **SATELLITE** view in the upper right corner. This will give you an idea of the terrain and surrounding.

4. [ ] For each of the caches you are interested in, click on the **SEND TO MY GPS** box near the top. This transfers the cache file from the web page to your GPS.

5. [ ] Once you have completed these steps you should have a few caches that are relatively close and for which you feel reasonably comfortable. This is what we call your geocaching **route**.

6. [ ] It's best to select about 5 caches in a row and expect that one or two of them might not be found. Send each of them to your GPS as described in step 4.

7. [ ] You may want to consider zooming in and out on the map so that it shows the caches you have selected, and then you can print the map off your computer. This will serve as a guide once you're out in the field. Write the cache name on the printout, as well as any hints or pointers you gathered from studying the cache description.

This procedure is the first of many route plans you will be creating in your geocaching career. If you are working with a group of geocachers they often trade turns in creating the geocaching route.

The next step is to go out into the field and search for the caches. Each trip searching for caches adds to your experience in finding them. You will start to learn the tricks of the trade, such as caches hidden in removable fence post covers, or very common *hangers* where a jar is covered in tape and left hanging on a tree branch. You will also learn how often the ***tools of the trade*** come in handy. These are devices such as a thin stick with a magnet on the end, a telescoping pole to help reach high caches, or a set of tweezers to extract the rolled up log inside a tiny container. Try to plan your trip so that you do not waste a lot of time searching for one cache. A common rule is to search no more than 20 minutes; then you can decide to move on to the next one.

Finally, when you come back, log your finds onto the Geocaching web page. Your log should record your experience and if necessary pass on information to the cachers who will follow you. If the log paper is almost full, for example, make a note of that in your report.

Now you're getting into the swing of geocaching. The next chapter is designed to broaden your experience by examining the variety of geocache types. Although traditional caches are the most popular, some of the other cache types are really fun to explore.

In the field

Once you are in the field with your GPS you have to click the buttons to view the caches that are closest to you. (Now you see why it was so important to read the manual!)

If you have a map, either in your head or printed on paper, then go to the route that leads you to the desired cache. The GPS device will indicate which direction to travel and how far away it is. Many GPS devices show the street you are on and a different colored line indicating which way you are supposed to walk.

As you get closer to the ground zero, very often an alarm will sound and you will see the cache icon on your GPS screen. Once in range of the cache you start looking around for the right hiding spot. Many GPS devices let you enter Found or Did Not Find on your device. You can also look up hints and past logs to help you find the cache.

9. A Variety of Cache Types

Cache types

Up until this point our focus has been on traditional caches. There are many other cache types that provide really exciting and unusual adventures. Here we will examine some of the variations on the traditional cache type.

Figure 14. Each cache type has its own icon. From left to right: Traditional cache, multi-cache, unknown cache, event cache, letterbox hybrid, Earthcache, virtual cache, CITO cache, mega event, and Wherigo.

Event caches

By far the most delightful cache type is the Event Cache. These are group gatherings where you can meet other geocachers in your area, find friends, exchange travel bugs, and have a good time. In addition, it all counts as a cache that you can log just as if you had found a cache container.

Event caches often include food, a group activity, or a public service, such as cleaning up a park. Event caches are HIGHLY RECOMMENDED activities, as it broadens your horizons and it's very entertaining.

Event caches allow you to share experiences with like-minded adventurers.

A good example is the Flash Mob event, where people gather secretly at a public place, then on signal they do something silly, like sing a song, then disperse (after signing the event log).

There are different ways to find events in your area. When you sign up with Geocaching.com you automatically receive monthly bulletins which list upcoming events. Event caches also appear on the area maps (**Figure 8** for example) as a little yellow dialog bubble. See **Figure 14** for cache type icons.

Step-by-Step:
Selecting event caches

If you want to search for them on Geocaching.com, follow these steps.

1. [ ] Go on line and navigate to Geocaching.com.

2. [ ] Click on the **COMMUNITY** tab (see **Figure 1**) and select Events.

3. [ ] Scroll down towards the bottom of the page and you will see a **CALENDAR OF EVENTS**.

4. [ ] For the day you are interested in, click on the date number at the top of the column.

5. [ ] International events are listed first. Scroll down to your state and click on the events in your area to read about them.

Step-by-Step:
Selecting specific cache types

Another, more focused way of finding specific cache types in your area:

1. [ ] Click on the **PLAY** tab and select **HIDE AND SEEK A CACHE**.

2. [ ] Near the bottom of the page in the left column, look for the words **TRY ADVANCED SEARCH OPTIONS**. Click on that.

3. [ ] In the Search for box, use the pull down menu labeled **ALL EVENT CACHES**. You will see a list of the different cache types you can choose. Use this procedure to select the types of caches you are interested in; that is besides Event Caches. You might want to check Virtual Caches as well while you're at it.

4. [ ] In the next box (**BY**) enter your Zip Code.

5. [ ] Click on the **SEARCH FOR GEOCACHES** box.

6. [ ] All the selected cache types in your area will show up on a map.

7. [ ] Click on and examine the ones you might be interested in.

8. [ ] Write the date and location down on your calendar if you select event caches, or load the cache into your GPS unit.

Be prepared to have some fun! Each cache type has its own symbol which appears on the map view. Again, see **Figure 14**.

Traditional caches

Traditional caches have been discussed already.

Geocaching.com defines it as follows: "This is the original geocache type consisting of, at minimum, a container and a log book or logsheet. Larger containers generally include items for trade. **Nano** or **Micro** caches are tiny containers that only hold a logsheet. The coordinates listed on the traditional cache page provide the geocache's exact location."

Multi-cache

A multi-cache has different parts or stages. At the first stage you find instructions or clues to the next stage. This repeats until you come to the last stage where the actual cache and log are located. Some multi-caches have only two steps. Some of them have coordinates for the next phase while others list instructions, such as "Follow the brick path until you see a large tree stump."

Virtual cache

A virtual cache does not have a physical container or a log to sign. Instead, you travel to the location and make the observations required by the cache web page. A virtual cache might be a physical structure, such as a roller coaster, or a statue of a great person, and you are required to record specific information to prove that you visited the site. As an example, the statue might have a commemorative plaque attached which tells you who the sculptor was, what date the statue was put in place, and who helped place it there.

Virtual caches are being phased out, so no new ones of this type will appear in the future.

Letterbox hybrid cache

Letterboxing is a sport which is very similar to geocaching, although you don't need a GPS unit for letterboxing. The Letterbox is a hidden box that you find, like a treasure hunt, by following a set of instructions. This hobby is so similar to geocaching that the Letterboxes that are registered as caches are called Letterbox Hybrid Caches. They are often geared towards younger players, although adults generally enjoy the activity just as much. Letterbox caches usually have more than one stage to complete before you find the final treasure.

The web presence for letterboxing is located at http://www.letterboxing.org/. The hobby of letterboxing generally includes making or buying a personal rubber stamp and ink pad. When you find the letterbox you are supposed to impress your stamp onto the log book inside the letterbox. You also can record the rubber stamp that is inside the letterbox to your own log book of stamp impressions that you carry with you. This way both you and the letterbox owner have a large collection of stamp impressions.

Unknown (puzzle) cache

Unknown caches generally involve a puzzle or riddle that you have to solve to find the cache. This category of caches includes a wide variety of head-scratching games, quizzes, and tricks that you have to figure out to find the cache location. This is, if you'll pardon the pun, a catch-all category for geocaches.

Puzzle caches are really fun and will keep your mind active. Most are pretty easy to solve but some can be quite difficult.

Example 1: You are sent to a starting point where you have to look around and find the street address of the nearest building. You are instructed to add the street number to the West coordinates of the starting point, and then subtract the same number from the North coordinates. The new coordinates point to where the cache is located.

Example 2. The puzzle cache name is Goblet of Fire, one of the Harry Potter books. You are asked "What age was Harry when he learned he was a wizard?" and "What is the 'Age of Majority' in the wizarding world?" These answers can be found by reading the book or checking the Goblet of Fire Wikipedia site on the internet. (The answers are 11 and 17 respectively.) You are then instructed to walk exactly 11 feet in one direction and 17 feet in another direction to find the actual cache site.

Earth cache

An Earth Cache is very similar to a virtual cache in that there is no container or log to sign. Similarly, you have to record specific information to prove you visited the site. As the name implies Earth Cache sites have geological or environmental significance which is quite often tremendously interesting. An Earth Cache might be at a fish hatchery or a meteor impact site. The information is generally available from signs, posters, or information booths at the site.

Miscellaneous cache types

There are several other cache types that are not as popular as the ones listed above. Meanwhile, Geocaching.com will sometimes add or delete a cache category. The ones that are rarely used or hard to find are:

Project APE caches: Caches with Planet of the Apes theme.

Webcam caches: A cache where you appear on a public web camera and someone records your visit. Webcam caches are being phased out, so no new ones of this type will appear in the future.

GPS adventures exhibit: GPS Adventures Mazes are designed to teach people of all ages about GPS technology and geocaching through interactive science experiences.

Wherigo caches: Wherigo is a stand-alone device using game cartridges for creating and playing GPS-enabled adventures in the real world.

For the latest information on cache types see: http://www.geocaching.com/about/cache_types.aspx.

10. The Journeyman Geocacher

Advancing from beginner to experienced geocacher

This book is designed to get you started in geocaching. If you've completed the previous chapters you are probably getting to know how to play the game. The biggest booster to the hobby is to join other geocachers, and attend geocaching events to improve your caching skills.

The best teacher is experience. As the number count of your found caches increases you will come across more complex caches, unusual hiding places, and creative cache containers. If you have any trouble, don't be shy to contact other geocachers who have found the cache that you may be having trouble with.

Geocaching is a wide open sport and things are changing every day. A good source for answering technical questions is the Geocaching Learn page, the first tab on the main page. See: http://www.geocaching.com/guide/.

Another good source, and a place to ask questions, is the Geocaching.com discussion forum which is handled by Groundspeak. See: http://forums.groundspeak.com/GC//.

Videos can also teach you a lot about geocaching. There are videos on geocaching at http://www.geocaching.com/videos/. You may also find a wide range of tutorials and adventures on popular video websites such as YouTube.com.

Circulating your own travel bugs

After geocaching for a while maybe you've been lucky enough to find a travel bug in one of the caches. These are little figurines, toys, or gadgets that have a travel bug coin, tag, or marker with a serial number used to track the object. The idea is to keep the item moving from cache to cache. If you own one you can look up a map of all the places the bug has traveled to. Actually, you can view the map of any travel bug for which you have the tracking number.

To view the page for any travel bug, simply enter Geocaching.com, select Play, and click on the FIND

TRAVEL BUGS listing in the pull-down menu. Enter the tracking number in the box labeled **ENTER THE TRACKING CODE OF THE ITEM** and press return.

About the center of the page you'll see the **VIEW MAP** link. When you click on that you will see a map of all the caches this particular travel bug has visited.

Now imagine if this were your own travel bug! You might drop it off while on vacation in another state, and you can see where it goes and who retrieved it.

To get started with *trackable items* you first have to buy a *travel bug*. They are sometimes referred to as *travel tags, geocoins*, or simply trackables: see **Figure 15**. Different companies produce and sell them. You can find travel bug sales on Geocaching.com by selecting the **SHOPPING** tab.

You will see a new page with **TRACKABLES** as one of the new tabs, near the center of the top of the page.

Figure 15. Travel Bugs and trackable items come in all shapes and sizes.

You can also find trackable items for sale at other websites. For example:

- http://www.coinsandpins.com/
- http://www.cacheboxstore.com/
- http://www.gpscity.com/
- http://www.thecachestation.com/categories/Travel-Tags/
- http://www.mygeogear.com/

Once you've purchased a trackable item you have to register it with Geocaching.com in order to create a tracking page. Some trackable items provide the activation code packaged with the item. For other distributors, such as CoinsAndPins.com you can retrieve the tracking code at the seller's web site. This is called activating the trackable. It then links you to the Geocaching.com site so you can register it there.

To *register a travel bug*, navigate to Geocaching.com; click on **PLAY** and select **FIND TRACKABLES**, then enter the tracking code and the activation code in the appropriate boxes.

Once you've registered the trackables you have to fill out a Geocaching.com form which tells everyone what the mission of the trackable is. You may want to upload a photo of the item too.

When the paperwork is done you can drop the trackable item off at any cache that is large enough to hold it. After registering, the trackable is automatically added to your personal inventory on Geocaching.com. Then, when you log your cache visit, you will see a box near the bottom of the cache page where you can check **DROPPED OFF**. The cache page will then show your trackable in its cache inventory on the right side of the page.

After that you simply check your trackables page to see when and where it has traveled. Every time someone moves your item you will receive an email notification. Have fun!

Hiding your own caches

Hiding your own cache is actually an advanced subject, but once you get into the swing of geocaching, sooner or later you will want to hide your own cache.

Be advised, you should have found at least 100 caches from other people before you start thinking of hiding your own. Since this is complex process and not for beginners we will list only a broad outline of the steps.

1. Create your cache container. Start simple. Bison tubes, which you can buy at many of the suppliers listed in the Appendix make great containers. Consider using a plastic film canister or covering a washed out mayonnaise jar with duct tape for your first container.

2. Take photographs of your container and the place where you expect to hide it. In order to post a picture to the Geocaching.com site you must have a direct link to the photo. Some, but not all photo hosting websites will provide the direct link for you. Photobucket.com is a popular example.

3. On Geocaching.com click on **PLAY** and select **HIDE AND SEEK A CACHE**. The **HIDE A CACHE** box on the right includes several links to help you get started. Be sure to read and understand the **CACHE LISTING REQUIREMENTS AND GUIDELINES** link. The hardest part is finding an area to hide your cache that is 1/10-th mile or more from any surrounding caches.

4. Once you are ready with your cache, your description, the location coordinates, and your photos, you can fill out the **ONLINE FORM** by clicking on that link. You may fill out most of it and come back later to complete the process.

Exploring beyond Geocaching.com

Although Geocaching.com is by far the most popular website for geocaching enthusiasts, there are many other sites that center around geocaching and GPS related activities. Some of these are listed below.

1. **Waymarking** is similar to virtual caches on Geocaching.com. Waymarks are sights and locations that you find with a GPS device and log your visits on line. Generally you must take a photograph to prove you visited the site. See http://www.waymarking.com/default.aspx?f=1.

2. **Navicache** is a site similar to Geocaching.com. They have different icons and require a separate sign-in. See http://www.navicache.com/.

3. **Terracaching** is also similar to Geocaching.com. The Terracaching site lists caches that are not necessarily listed with other sites. For example Geocaching caches are required to be a tenth of a mile distant from each other, but there may be a Terracache very close to a Geocaching.com location. See http://www.Terracaching.com.

4. **Open Caching.** Opencaching, like Terracaching is independent of Geocaching.com, so some caches may be listed here that are not on other sites, and they too may be closer than 1/10th mile from caches on Geocaching.com.
See: http://www.opencaching.us/index.php.

5. **GPSgames** offers several activities that rely on your GPS unit. There are games such as Geodashing, Geogolf, and Shutterspot. An example from their website:
"Shutterspot is a game in which some players take photographs and other players are challenged to find the exact spot where the photographer stood when the camera shutter clicked. That's the 'Shutterspot'."
See: http://www.gpsgames.org.

6. **Earthcache** is a site dedicated to Earthcaches and is a partner with Geocaching.com. See: http://www.earthcache.org/.

7. **Handicaching** is a site for the handicapped or those who want low difficulty caches. Caches are ranked by users for terrain and accessibility.
See: http://www.handicaching.com/.

Appendix

Geocaching websites

THE major site for geocaching is Geocaching.com, the largest and most respected resource for this hobby. They also have an excellent discussion forum at forums.groundspeak.com/GC/.

Groundspeak is the umbrella organization for Geocaching.com, Waymarking.com (virtual caches), Wherigo.com, and CITO, the Cache-In, Trash Out adjunct to geocaching.

These interconnected website URLs are as follows

- http://www.geocaching.com/
- http://www.groundspeak.com/
- http://www.waymarking.com/

Geocaching-related websites

Garmin:
http://www8.garmin.com/outdoor/geocaching/

Buxleys Geocaching Waypoint:
http://brillig.com/geocaching/

Open Caching: http://www.opencaching.com/en/

TerraCaching: http://www.terracaching.com/

Letterboxing: http://www.letterboxing.org

http://www.handicaching.com/

http://www.navicache.com/

http://www.waymarking.com/default.aspx?f=1

http://www.GPSGames.org

http://www.Earthcache.org

Magazines

- FTF Geocacher: http://www.ftfgeocacher.com/
- Online Geocacher: http://onlinegeocacher.com/

Major manufacturers

- DeLorme: http://www.delorme.com/
- Garmin: http://www.garmin.com/us/
- Lowrance: http://www.lowrance.com/Products/Outdoor/
- Magellan: http://www.magellangps.com/

Discussion forums

- Groundspeak: http://gpsunderground.com/forum/forum.php
- GPS Passion: http://www.gpspassion.com/forumsen/
- GPS Review: http://forums.gpsreview.net/

Geocaching supplies, pins, travel bugs, and containers

- http://www.coinsandpins.com/
- http://www.cacheboxstore.com/
- http://www.gpscity.com/
- http://www.thecachestation.com/categories/Travel-Tags/
- http://www.mygeogear.com/

Other books by Vince Migliore

Creative Cache Containers for Geocaching, ISBN-13 # 978-1477635711, available at Amazon.com.

Metal Detecting for the Beginner, ISBN-13 # 978-1452862453, available at Amazon.com.

Index

Notes

Printed in Great Britain
by Amazon.co.uk, Ltd.,
Marston Gate.